T0387380

Greetings, jaguars!

JAGUARS

QUINN M. ARNOLD

CREATIVE EDUCATION | CREATIVE PAPERBACKS

4

table of contents

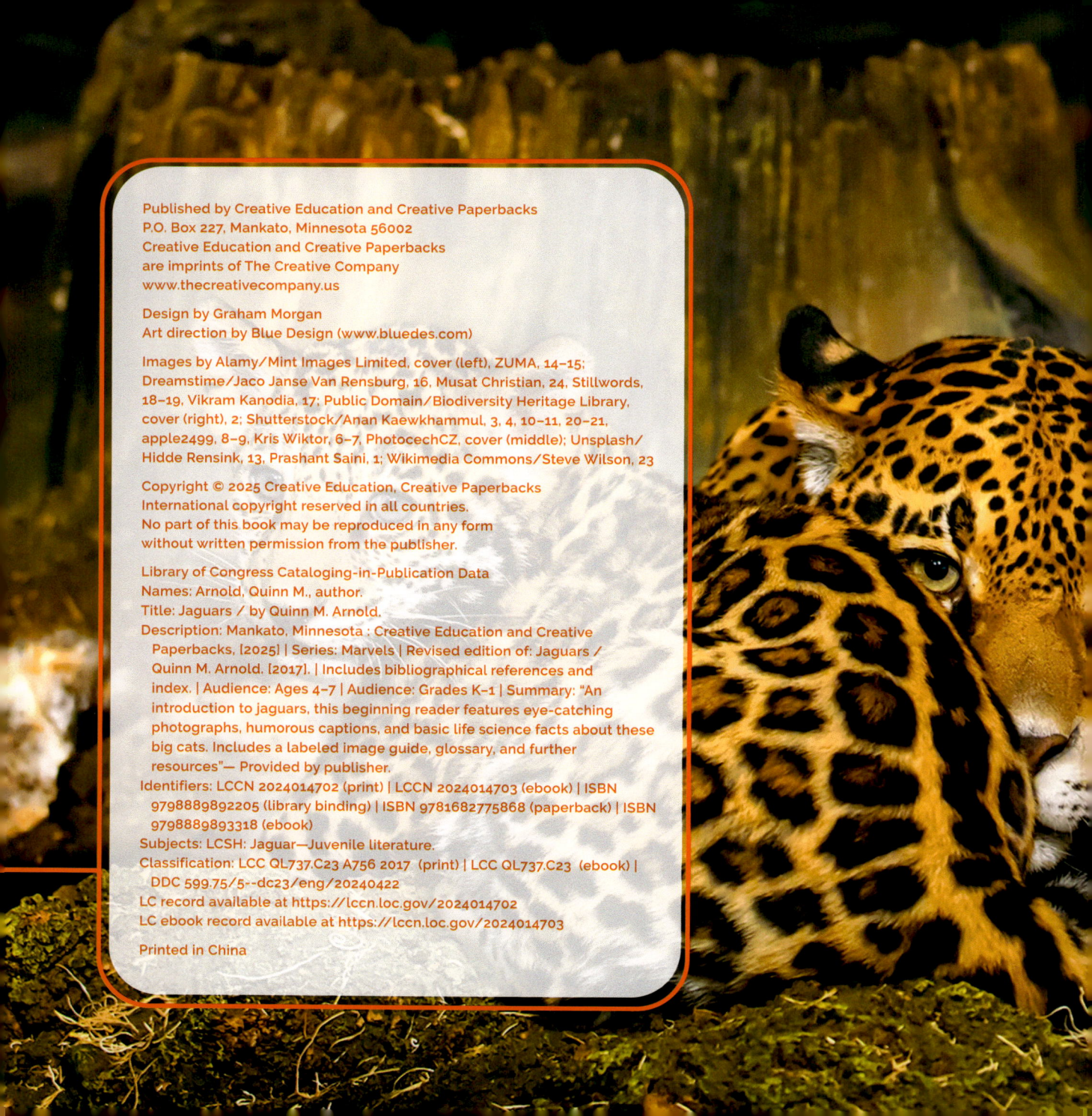

Published by Creative Education and Creative Paperbacks
P.O. Box 227, Mankato, Minnesota 56002
Creative Education and Creative Paperbacks
are imprints of The Creative Company
www.thecreativecompany.us

Design by Graham Morgan
Art direction by Blue Design (www.bluedes.com)

Images by Alamy/Mint Images Limited, cover (left), ZUMA, 14–15; Dreamstime/Jaco Janse Van Rensburg, 16, Musat Christian, 24, Stillwords, 18–19, Vikram Kanodia, 17; Public Domain/Biodiversity Heritage Library, cover (right), 2; Shutterstock/Anan Kaewkhammul, 3, 4, 10–11, 20–21, apple2499, 8–9, Kris Wiktor, 6–7, PhotocechCZ, cover (middle); Unsplash/Hidde Rensink, 13, Prashant Saini, 1; Wikimedia Commons/Steve Wilson, 23

Library of Congress Cataloging-in-Publication Data
Names: Arnold, Quinn M., author.
Title: Jaguars / by Quinn M. Arnold.
Description: Mankato, Minnesota : Creative Education and Creative Paperbacks, [2025] | Series: Marvels | Revised edition of: Jaguars / Quinn M. Arnold. [2017]. | Includes bibliographical references and index. | Audience: Ages 4–7 | Audience: Grades K–1 | Summary: "An introduction to jaguars, this beginning reader features eye-catching photographs, humorous captions, and basic life science facts about these big cats. Includes a labeled image guide, glossary, and further resources"— Provided by publisher.
Identifiers: LCCN 2024014702 (print) | LCCN 2024014703 (ebook) | ISBN 9798889892205 (library binding) | ISBN 9781682775868 (paperback) | ISBN 9798889893318 (ebook)
Subjects: LCSH: Jaguar—Juvenile literature.
Classification: LCC QL737.C23 A756 2017 (print) | LCC QL737.C23 (ebook) | DDC 599.75/5--dc23/eng/20240422
LC record available at https://lccn.loc.gov/2024014702
LC ebook record available at https://lccn.loc.gov/2024014703

Printed in China

Jaguars are big cats. They are the biggest cats in the Americas. Most jaguars live in **rainforests**.

7

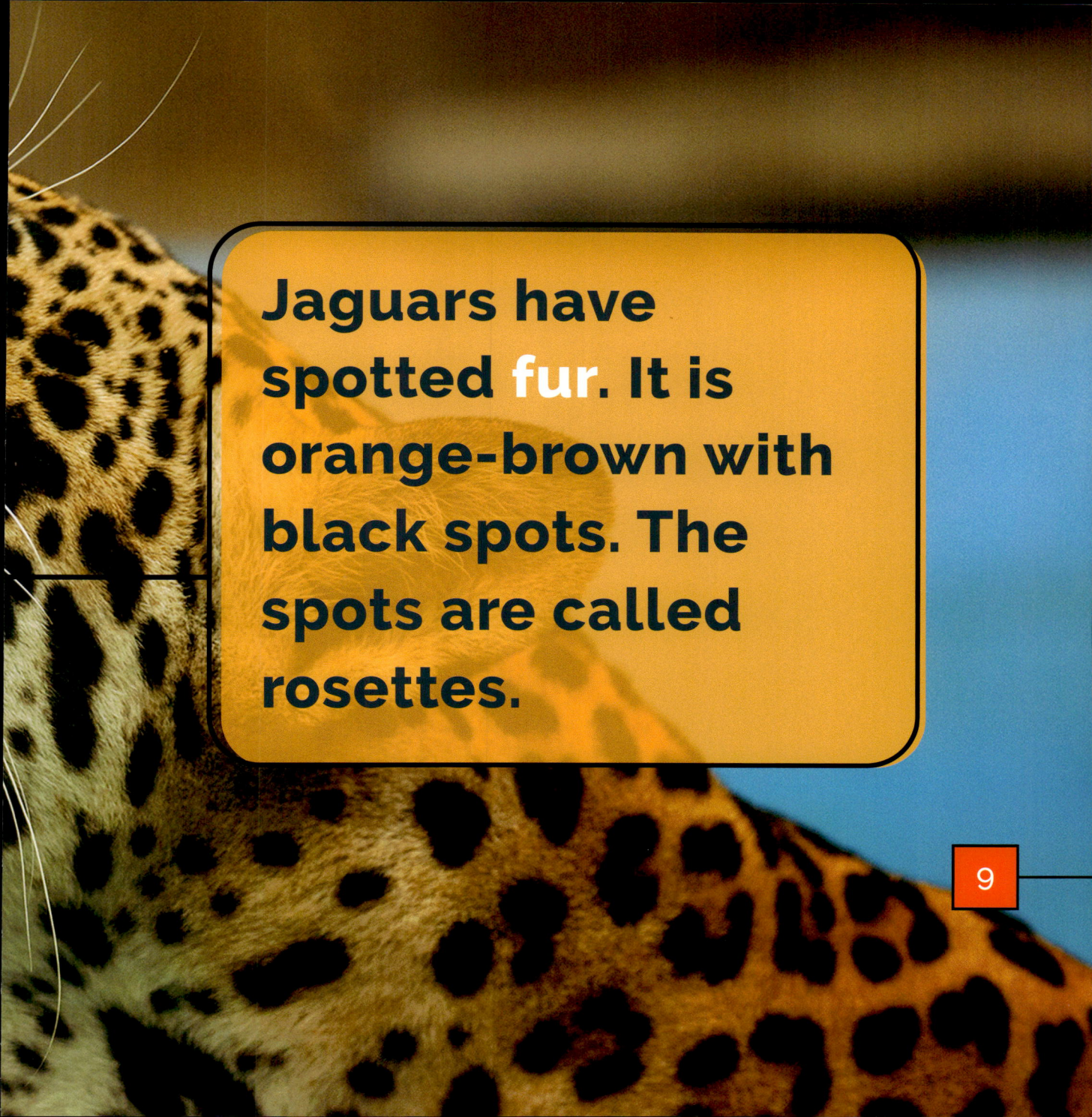

Jaguars have spotted **fur**. It is orange-brown with black spots. The spots are called rosettes.

9

A jaguar's tail is long. Jaguar legs are short but strong. They can leap far!

A JAGUAR'S COAT HELPS IT HIDE.

11

A jaguar eats meat. It waits for prey. Then it jumps!

13

14

JAGUAR MOTHERS HAVE ONE TO FOUR CUBS AT A TIME.

Baby jaguars are called cubs. Cubs live with their mother. They play and learn to hunt.

15

Jaguars sleep for most of the day. They go swimming. They look for food at night.

17

Farewell, jaguars!

[Picture a Jaguar]

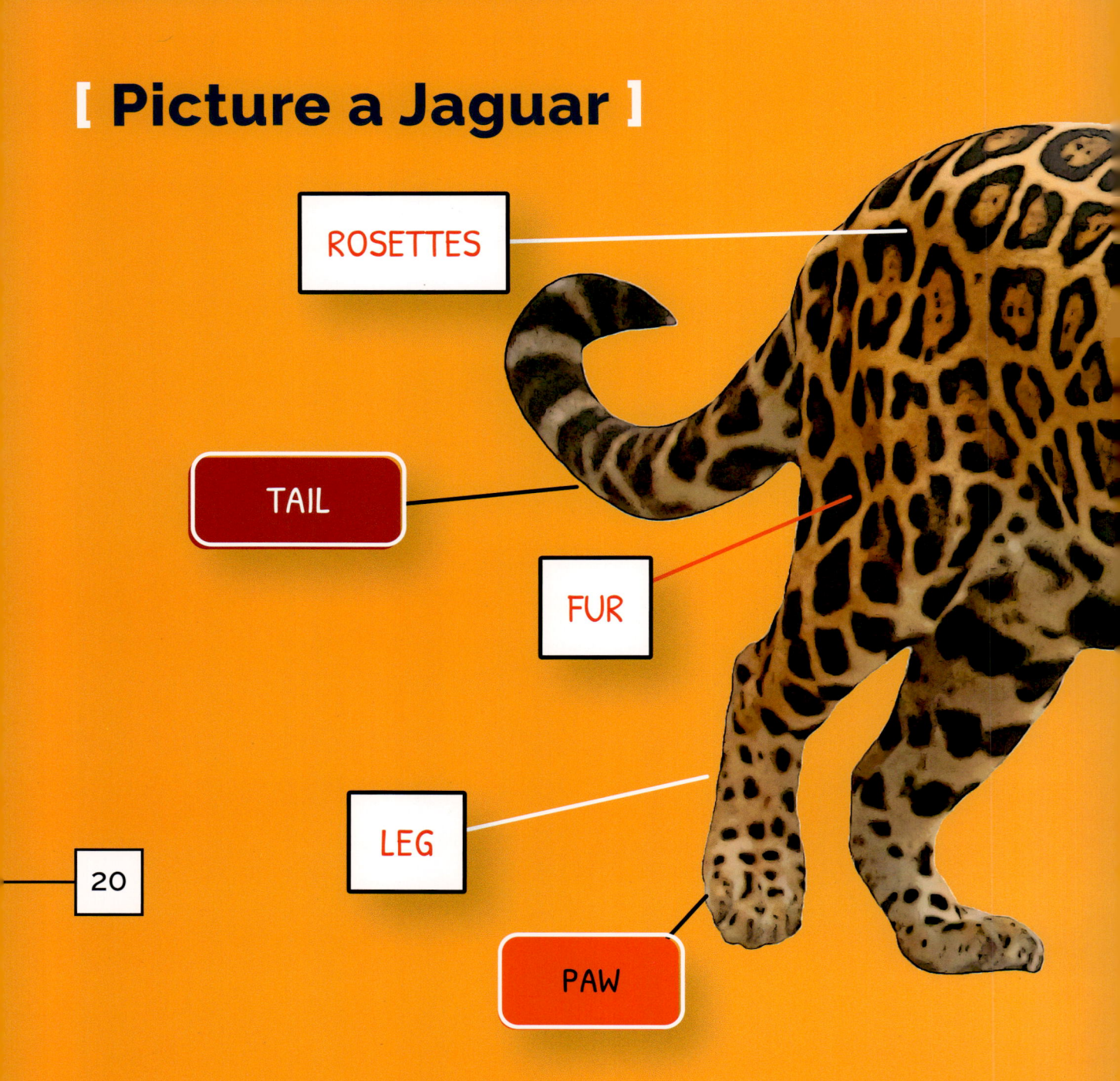

ROSETTES

TAIL

FUR

LEG

20

PAW

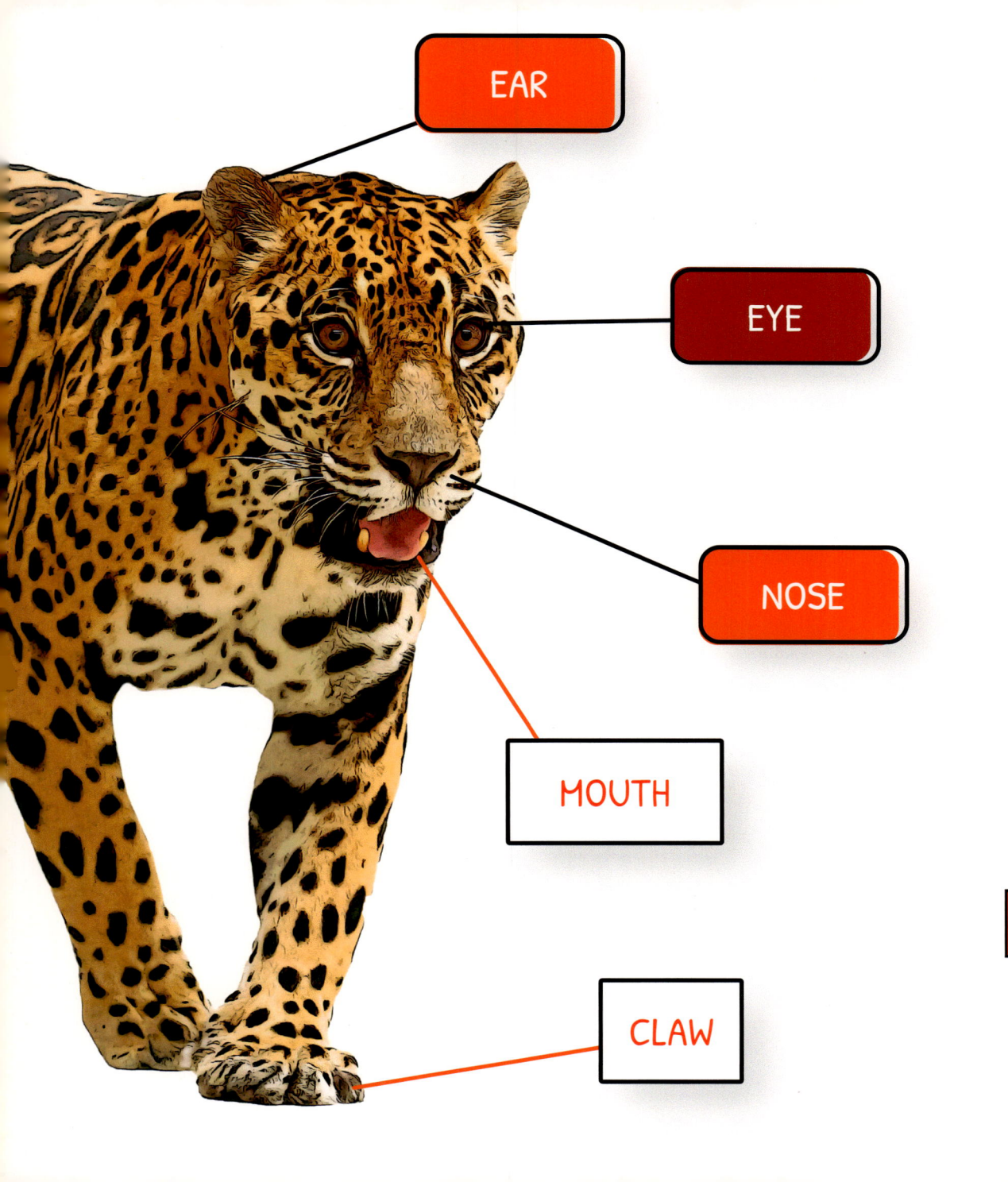

EAR

EYE

NOSE

MOUTH

CLAW

21

WORDS TO KNOW

fur: the short, hairy coat of an animal

prey: animals that are eaten by other animals

rainforest: forest that gets a lot of rain

READ MORE

Klepeis, Alicia. *Jaguars*. Minneapolis: Bellwether Media, 2024.

Leavitt, Amie Jane. *Awesome Animals of South America*. Mount Joy, Penn.: Curious Fox Books, 2024.

WEBSITES

Britannica Kids: Jaguar https://kids.britannica.com/students/article/jaguar/275122

An introduction to the biggest cat in North America, the jaguar.

Jaguar https://sdzwildlifeexplorers.org/animals/jaguar

Fun facts about the jaguar from the San Diego Zoo.

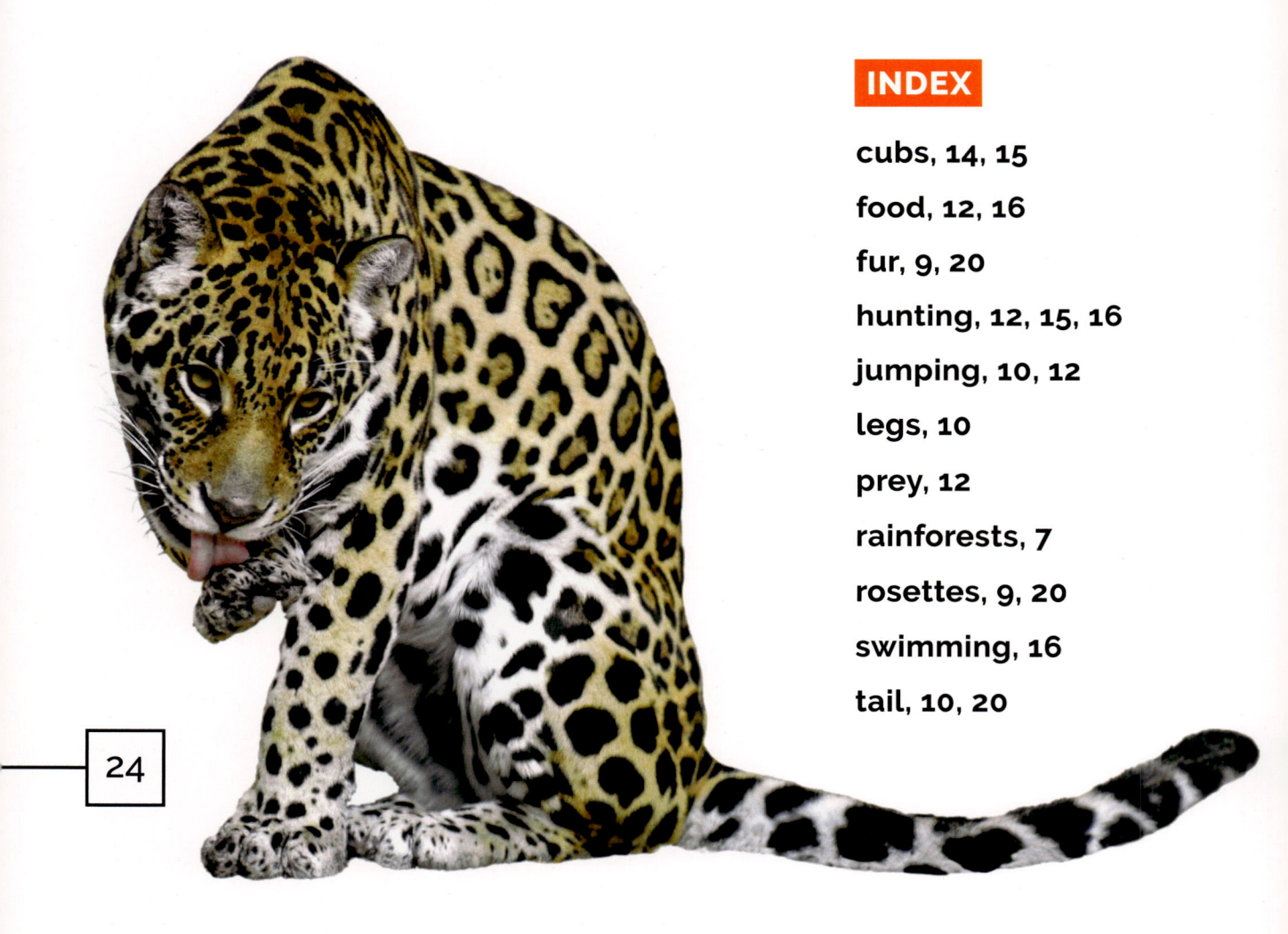